Pop,
You're "Poifect!"

Other Three Stooges® Gift Books

"Why, I Oughta . . ." Wish You a Happy Birthday!:
A Three Stooges Birthday Toast

Pop, You're "Poifect!"

A Three Stooges Salute to Dad

**Andrews McMeel
Publishing**

Kansas City

Pop, You're "Poifect!"

www.threestooges.com

ISBN: 0-7407-2688-9

Library of Congress Control Number: 2002103677

02 03 04 05 06 TWP 10 9 8 7 6 5 4 3 2 1

Attention: Schools and Businesses

Andrews McMeel books are available at quantity discounts with bulk purchase for educational, business, or sales promotional use. For information, please write to: Special Sales Department, Andrews McMeel Publishing, 4520 Main Street, Kansas City, Missouri 64111.

Hey there, Pops! Wanna hear a shocker?

I've been thinking about you a lot lately ...

and about what a lucky duck I am
to have you as my dad.

I realize I wasn't always the easiest kid to raise.

I know that there were nights
when I kept you awake with worry

and days I probably made you pull out your hair
in frustration (especially grade-card days).

I admit that occasionally I gave you good reason to get downright steamed.

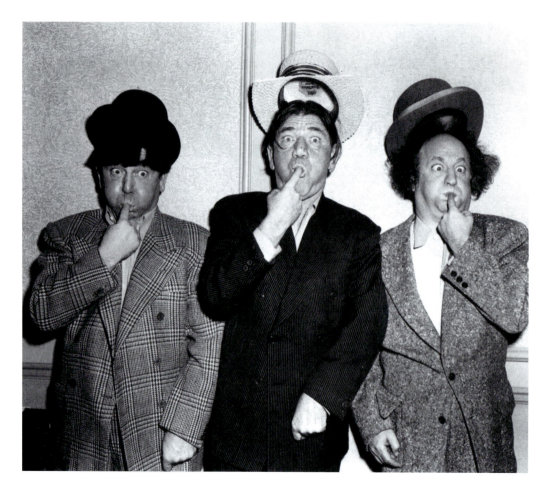

(And frankly, I'm amazed that you
didn't blow up more often.)

But somehow, we all survived the perils of my reckless youth.

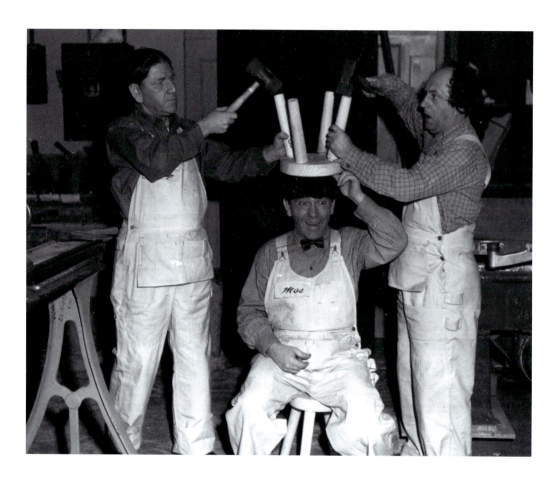

And your level-headed guidance
was one of the biggest reasons.

You see, even though you didn't think
I was watching or listening, I *did* pay attention
to the example you set.

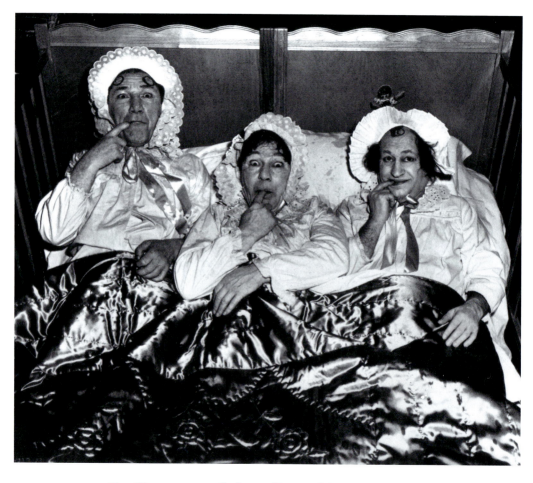

And everything I really needed
to know about growing up,

I learned by watching you.

**You taught me to surround myself
with true friends,**

the importance of making
a good first impression,

how to handle myself in the great outdoors,

and how to behave myself in fancy restaurants.

You taught me how to work hard
without complaining

and how to handle money wisely.

Not to mention the manly arts of shaving . . .

and parallel parking.

You taught me early in life
that if you face up to your fears ...

everything will be all right in the end.

And you taught me that if a man doesn't stand for something . . .

he'll fall for anything.

From you, I learned how to treat women with the proper respect . . .

and the dangers of letting a pretty girl
come between friends.

Whether times were good or bad,
you were always there for me, Dad,

and ready to gently guide me
in the right direction.

**You taught me that it's not how many times
you get knocked down that counts . . .**

but how many times you get back up again.

You always encouraged me to follow my dreams,

no matter how crazy they
may have seemed to you.

You saw me through those awkward years
(which some would say have never ended),

**and hardly ever embarrassed me
in front of my friends (unlike some kids' dads).**

So, here's to you, Dad—

a man of many talents,

unquestionable integrity,

impeccable fashion sense,

uncommon wisdom,

and a sophisticated sense of humor.

Thanks for being my chauffeur,

my coach,

my chief adviser,

my protector and provider,

and my occasional **ATM.**

Thanks for always being in my corner.

Thanks for the times you held me back when I was about to do something stupid.

Thanks for letting me make some mistakes for my own good.

Let's face it, we can both be
a little hard-headed at times . . .

**but somehow you've always managed
to put up with my bull.**

So thanks for all the times you've bailed me out (not literally, of course—not yet),

and for all the times you've gone to any lengths
to cheer me up when I was down.

I know there may be hard knocks ahead,

but I know I'll always be okay
as long as you're behind me.

**And if I could choose any dad in the world,
it'd be no contest . . .**

I'd choose you in a second.

I swear!